RESPONSIBLE CITIZENSHIP

Voting

by Kirsten Chang

BELLWETHER MEDIA • MINNEAPOLIS, MN

Blastoff! Readers are carefully developed by literacy experts to build reading stamina and move students toward fluency by combining standards-based content with developmentally appropriate text.

Level 1 provides the most support through repetition of high-frequency words, light text, predictable sentence patterns, and strong visual support.

Level 2 offers early readers a bit more challenge through varied sentences, increased text load, and text-supportive special features.

Level 3 advances early-fluent readers toward fluency through increased text load, less reliance on photos, advancing concepts, longer sentences, and more complex special features.

★ **Blastoff! Universe**

Reading Level

Blastoff! Beginners — Grade **K**

Blastoff! READERS — Grades **1–3**

Blastoff! DISCOVERY — Grade **4**

This edition first published in 2022 by Bellwether Media, Inc.

No part of this publication may be reproduced in whole or in part without written permission of the publisher. For information regarding permission, write to Bellwether Media, Inc., Attention: Permissions Department, 6012 Blue Circle Drive, Minnetonka, MN 55343.

Library of Congress Cataloging-in-Publication Data

Names: Chang, Kirsten, 1991- author.
Title: Voting / by Kirsten Chang.
Description: Minneapolis, MN : Bellwether Media, Inc., 2022. | Series: Blastoff! Readers: Responsible citizenship | Includes bibliographical references and index. | Audience: Ages 5-8 | Audience: Grades K-1 | Summary: "Developed by literacy experts for students in kindergarten through grade three, this book introduces voting to young readers through leveled text and related photos"–Provided by publisher.
Identifiers: LCCN 2021016560 (print) | LCCN 2021016561 (ebook) | ISBN 9781644875018 (library binding) | ISBN 9781648344770 (paperback) | ISBN 9781648344091 (ebook)
Subjects: LCSH: Voting–Juvenile literature. | Presidents–Election–Juvenile literature.
Classification: LCC JF1001 .C46 2022 (print) | LCC JF1001 (ebook) | DDC 324.6/5–dc23
LC record available at https://lccn.loc.gov/2021016560
LC ebook record available at https://lccn.loc.gov/2021016561

Text copyright © 2022 by Bellwether Media, Inc. BLASTOFF! READERS and associated logos are trademarks and/or registered trademarks of Bellwether Media, Inc.

Editor: Kieran Downs   Designer: Brittany McIntosh

Printed in the United States of America, North Mankato, MN.

Table of Contents

It is **Election Day**. Maria is voting for president. She makes her choice!

What Is Voting?

Voting is a way to
make a choice.

VOTERS ENTER
HERE

ELECTORES ENTREN AQUÍ

VOTÈ M UNE PA ISIT

7

We **research**
our choices.
We vote for the
ones we like best.

9

We vote for leaders like presidents or mayors. We vote for laws.

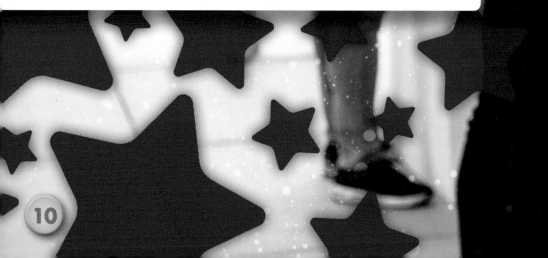

Adults vote at
public buildings.
They go to
town halls, schools,
and libraries.

VOTE HERE

Must Haves

- ✓ **United States citizen**
- ✓ **18 years old or older**

Voters mark their choices on **ballots**. Ballots can be on paper or a computer.

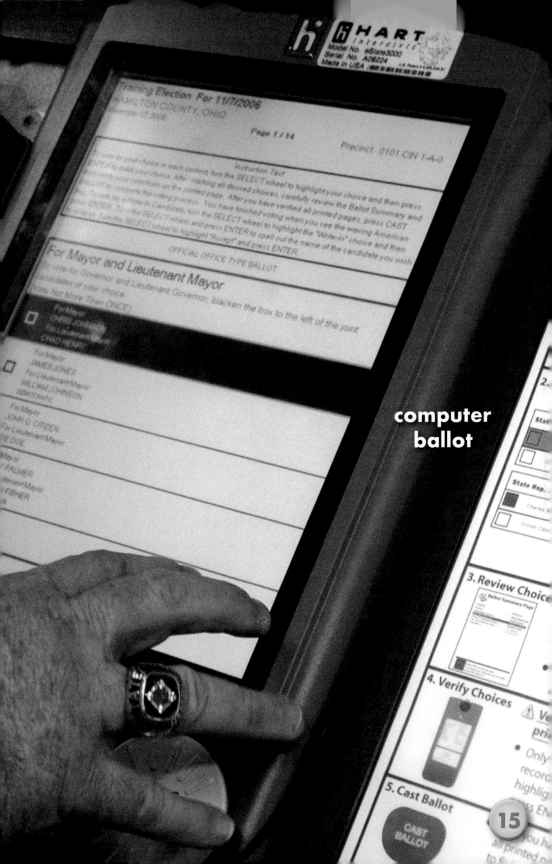

computer
ballot

The votes are counted.
We find out
the **results**!

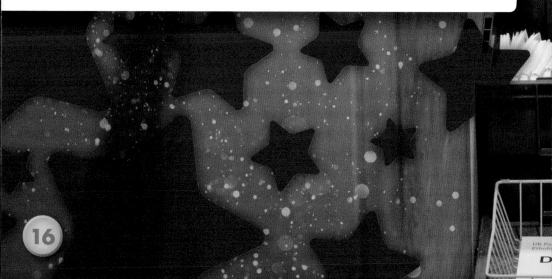

**counting
votes**

SLAUGHTER
Anthony David

WILLIAM

FUL BALLOT
APERS

Why Is Voting Important?

Voting can bring changes. It can make the world better.

POLLING PLACE
投票站 CASILLA ELECTORAL
投票所 LUGAR NG BOTOHAN
投票所 PHÒNG PHIẾU

With/Without

leaders are chosen

no choice of leaders

19

Voting makes our voices heard. It is part of being a good **citizen**!

Ballot

Question

Why do you think voting is important?

BALLOTS

Glossary

ballots

papers or computers where voters mark their choices

research

to search for informatio

citizen

someone who is a member of a certain city, state, or country

results

CONGRATULATIONS
President-Elect Biden

the answers at the end of an event

Election Day

VOTE HERE

the day when people vote

To Learn More

AT THE LIBRARY

Alexander, Vincent. *Voting: Being an Active Citizen*. Minneapolis, Minn.: Jump!, 2019.

Bonwill, Ann. *We Can Vote*. New York, N.Y.: Children's Press, 2019.

Kortuem, Amy. *Voting in Elections*. North Mankato, Minn.: Pebble, 2020.

ON THE WEB

FACTSURFER

Factsurfer.com gives you a safe, fun way to find more information.

1. Go to www.factsurfer.com.

2. Enter "voting" into the search box and click 🔍.

3. Select your book cover to see a list of related content.

Index

The images in this book are reproduced through the courtesy of: adamkaz, front cover, pp. 4-5; Jeffrey Isaac Greenberg 16+/ Alamy Stock Photo, pp. 6-7; Vicki Beaver/ Alamy Stock Photo, pp. 8-9; LPETTET, pp. 10-11; Andrey_Popov, pp. 12-13; ZUMA Press, Inc./ Alamy Stock Photo, pp. 14-15; ComposedPix, pp. 16-17; Hill Street Studios/ Getty Images, pp. 18-19; lev radin, p. 19 (left); Allan Ramsay/ Wikipedia, p. 19 (right); fstop123, pp. 20-21; The Toidi, p. 22 (ballots); Rawpixel.com, p. 22 (citizen); Trevor Bexon, p. 22 (Election Day); fizkes, p. 22 (research); Gottography, p. 22 (results).